GRAMMAR

RULES and PRACTICE 1

Susan J. Daughtrey M.Ed.

Childs World Education Limited
1995

CONTENTS

PARTS OF SPEECH

PARTS OF SPEECH

What exactly is meant by a *part of speech*?
We can compare a word in a sentence to a digit in a number.
In mathematics the value of a figure is determined by its place or position. We call this *place value*.
Let us consider the number: 4 4 4 4

Depending on where we place the digit 4 determines its value.
If we place 4 in the hundreds column, has a value 100 times greater than the same digit placed in the units column. 4 in the thousands column is 100 times greater than the same digit in the tens column or 1000 times greater that the 4 placed in the units column, and so on. In each case we are using the same digit. Even so, its *value* changes according to the position of the digit in the number.

And so it is with a word.
Depending upon where a word is placed in the sentence and hence the words surrounding it, determines the job it does and so its part of speech.
Take the word *swing* in this sentence:

I stand on the *swing*.

Here *the swing* is the name of an object. Here, *swing* is a common noun.
I stand is the name of the action. Here, *stand* is a verb.

Neither word has the same function in this sentence.

I *swing* on the stand.

I swing is the name of an action. Here it is a verb.
The stand is the name of the thing on which I swing. Here it is a common noun.

Change the position of the word (like the 4) in relation to the other words in the sentence, and in so doing, change its function, and you change its part of speech.

Some words have a prescribed (already determined) part of speech. However, it is only by analysis of the whole sentence can we be absolutely certain what part of speech a word is assuming. Like *swing*, it is possible for a word to change its part of speech depending on its position, the words that surround it, and the consequent job it is doing in the sentence. Here, for instance, *the* precedes *swing* in the first sentence. This suggests swing is the name of a thing, a *noun. I* precedes *swing* in the second sentence. *Swing* now becomes an action word, a *verb*. Now the same word *swing* affected by, and relating to, different words in the sentence, has a different function and hence a different part of speech.
We can see how this applies to many words.

Example:

The *hunting*(noun) of wild animals is deplorable.
The *hunting*(adj.) lodge was a welcome sight at the end of a long, tiring day.
I have been *hunting*(verb) everywhere for my pencil, and still can't find it.

The part of speech played by the word *hunting* in these sentences changes according to its position, the way it relates to the words around it, and its consequent function. It is a noun, an adjective or a verb depending on where it is placed and what job it is doing in the sentence. It is only then by analysis of the full sentence can we be certain of what part of speech a word is assuming at any one time. This is true for many words.

Mark(verb) the *centre*(noun) of the circle with a cross.
Mark(noun) *centred*(verb) the ball perfectly and a goal was scored.

But there are clues as to what part of speech a word is *likely* to be.
Its spelling often gives us a clue.
A word ending in *s* is *likely* to be a *plural noun*, or a *verb* in the *third* person singular.
Example:

The girl *carries*(verb) the *books*(noun) to school.

A word ending in *ly* is likely to be an *adverb* or possibly an adjective.
Example:

The *lovely*(adj.) lady spoke *politely*(adv.) to the children.

Words ending in *ness*, *hood*, *age*, *tion* and *dom*, are likely to be *abstract nouns*.
Example:

Happi*ness* in child*hood* and marri*age* is a condi*tion* which requires wis*dom*.

A word ending in *er* is likely to be a noun or an *adjective* or *adverb* in the *comparative* degree.
Example:

The *builder*(noun) will build *faster*(adv.) a *bigger*(adj.) and *better*(adj.) house.

A word ending in *est* is likely to be an *adjective* or *adverb* in the *superlative* degree.
Example:

The Capitol building in Washington, America, is the *tallest*(adj.) building in the city.

Besides spelling, the punctuation of the sentence complements grammar and helps us to determine what role a word might be playing in a sentence.

THE SENTENCE

In *Punctuation Rules and Practice 1*, we looked at the characteristics and the punctuation of the four types of sentence: the *statement*, *command*(*imperative*), *interrogative* and *exclamation*.We also defined a sentence as a sequence of words which articulates a complete and unified idea or thought and as such makes complete sense by itself and can stand alone. It needs no other words to help it.

Now we shall look at the grammatical features of our language, the internal structure of the sentence and the order and function of the words *within* the sentence to identify the rules for the proper usage of English.

A sentence *usually* has a subject (a person or thing which does the action of the verb), and a predicate (the remaining words in the sentence) which contains a finite verb (a verb which usually has a subject and a tense and tells you the main action occurring). If it is a *simple* sentence, that is all it contains.
Example:

The cat sat on the mat.

This is a *simple* sentence. It has one subject (cat) and one predicate which contains a finite verb (sat).
One could add adjectives:

The *long-haired, purring* cat sat on the *warm, red-coloured* mat.

and adverbs:

The long-haired, purring cat sat *quietly* and *patiently* on the warm, red-coloured mat.
But it would still be a *simple* sentence. It still contains one subject and a predicate with a finite verb.

If you used simple sentences all the time, your writing and speech would be very jerky, rather boring and uninteresting to read. You must join groups of words together to add variety, colour, interest to your writing and to make it flow.

By doing so, you will create **complex and compound sentences**.

COMPLEX and COMPOUND SENTENCES

A clause is a group of words which contains a verb. There are three types of clause: a main clause, a subordinate clause and a co-ordinating clause.

A Complex Sentence

A *main clause* is a group of words which contains a verb. It can be part of a sentence or, if it were given a capital letter and a final punctuation mark of its own, can stand alone as a sentence in its own right and make complete sense. It is the most important clause.

A *subordinate clause* has a verb but cannot stand alone as a sentence. It needs to be added to the main clause to make sense and be given meaning. A subordinate clause can act as a noun, an adjective, or an adverb depending on the job it does in the sentence.

A main clause and one or more subordinate clauses joined together make up a *complex* sentence.
Example:

Jane, who is fat, is my best friend.

Jane is my best friend is the main clause,
who is fat is a subordinate clause doing the job of an adjective describing Jane.
It is therefore a subordinate clause (it cannot stand alone as a sentence) and an adjectival clause. Adjectival clauses often begin with *who, which, that* or *whom*.

He missed the bus because he was late.
He missed the bus (main clause)
because he was late. (subordinate clause)

Because he was late is a subordinate clause acting as an adverb answering the
question *why* did he miss the bus? This is a subordinate clause and an adverbial
clause. An adverbial clause, like an adverb, answers the question, when? why? how?
where? does an action take place.

If the subordinate clause comes at the beginning of the sentence, it is separated from
the main clause by a comma. If the main clause comes first, a comma is not needed.

**Several subordinate clauses each doing a different job can be added to a
main clause.**
Example:
     Sara, who is pretty, says she will come when she finishes her homework.

Here, *Sara says she will come* is the main clause. *Who is pretty* is a subordinate
clause. It contains a verb but it cannot stand alone as a sentence in its own right. It is
only given meaning by being attached to the main clause. It *describes* Sara, therefore
it is an *adjectival clause. When she finishes her homework* is a subordinate clause with
a verb which answers the question *when will she come*? It is therefore an *adverbial
clause of time*.

In the example above, the adjectival clause is separated from the main clause by
commas, but the adverbial clause does not need to be separated because it follows the
main clause. (see *Punctuation Rules and Practice 1*)

A Compound Sentence

A compound sentence is made up of two or more co-ordinating clauses joined
together by a co-ordinating conjunction or separated from each other by a comma or
semi-colon.

Co-ordinating clauses are of equal status. They do not describe or add meaning to each
other as does a subordinate clause to a main clause. Rather each co-ordinating clause
could stand as a simple sentence in its own right.

Punctuation of a compound sentence is very important. (see *Punctuation Rules and
Practice 1 and 2*.) When using a conjunction, there is a comma if the subject of each
co-ordinating clause is different.
Example:
     Susie likes to sew, *but* John prefers to read.

Here two co-ordinating clauses of equal status are joined together with the co-
ordinating conjunction *but* and a comma separates them because the subject of each
clause is different. If the subject remains the same, no comma is necessary.
     The ship hit a rock *and* sank to the bottom of the sea.

A conjunction *and* commas can be used.

John likes to read, Susie likes to sew, *but* Chris prefers to do nothing at all.

A semi-colon can take the place of a conjunction. It has the effect of re-establishing the two co-ordinating clauses as simple sentences.

The ship hit a rock; it sank to the bottom of the sea.

A Phrase

A phrase is a group of words which does not contain a verb, does not make sense by itself and could never stand alone as a sentence. A phrase is a group of words which forms part of a clause or sentence. Without the other words in the sentence, a phrase has no sensible meaning.

A phrase could be used instead of a single adjective, noun or adverb.
Example:

...up the hill...   ...in a week or two...

Each of these could take the place of a single adverb answering the question where? or when? A *subject* and a *verb* would have to be added to these words for them to make sense.
Example:

The boy (subject) walked (verb) *up the hill.*
(*adverbial phrase* answering the question *where?*)

Example:

The au pair (subject) will be visiting (verb) London *in a week or two.*
(*adverbial phrase* of time answering the question *when?*)

A *noun phrase* takes the place of a noun:
Example:

All the pupils in year eight (noun phrase) are expected to come.
Here, the *noun phrase* is acting as the subject of the sentence.

It can be seen then, that by adding different types of phrase and clause to a simple sentence, you are able to enrich your language and convey more precise information. Colour, interest, variety and texture can be added to your essays and compositions. However, care must be taken with punctuation.

A sentence is a group of words which begins with a capital letter
and ends with a full stop, exclamation mark or question mark.
It makes complete sense by itself and can stand alone.
It usually has a *subject* and a *predicate* with a *finite verb*.

> **A clause** has a finite verb and is either part of a sentence (main, subordinate and co-ordinating clauses) or, in the case of a main clause only, could stand alone and act as a sentence in its own right (given a capital letter and full stop of its own).
> A *subordinate clause* does the work of an adjective, adverb or noun.
> *Co-ordinating clauses* are of equal status.
>
> **A phrase** can never stand alone as a sentence and must be joined to other words (clauses and sentences) to be given meaning.
> It does not contain a verb.
> It can act as a noun, adjective or adverb.

There are eight parts of speech:

1.	The Noun	5.	The Adverb
2.	The Adjective	6.	The Conjunction
3.	The Pronoun	7.	The Preposition
4.	The Verb	8.	The Interjection

Every word in the English language, depending upon its function, falls into one of these categories. We shall look at each part of speech in detail in this and *Grammar Rules and Practice 2* in this series. The explanation of each part of speech will be summarised and immediately followed by practice exercises for you to complete – to practise and revise each grammar topic. At the back of each book there are Rule Summaries for you to complete and copy onto index cards. These will serve as your own revision reference system to which you can refer at any time in the future.

In addition to these topics, we shall look at the definite and indefinite article, gender of nouns, families and forming the singular and plural of nouns.

THE NOUN

> **A word, or group of words (phrases and clauses) that tells us the *name* of a person, animal, place or thing is a *noun*.**

There are four types of noun:

1.	Common nouns.	3.	Collective nouns.
2.	Proper nouns.	4.	Abstract nouns.

THE COMMON NOUN

Common nouns are the *ordinary* names given to different kinds of people, places, animals or things.

Example:

PEOPLE	**PLACES**	**ANIMALS**	**THINGS**
boy	school	tiger	pencil
girl	cinema	mouse	ruler
teacher	garden	cat	table
doctor	park	dog	book

Common nouns do not begin with a capital letter.

PRACTICE : THE COMMON NOUN

Exercise One:

Underline the *common nouns* in the following sentences.

1. On the table there was a knife, a fork, a spoon, a plate and a dish.

2. The girl came out of the shop carrying six parcels in a paper bag.

3. The teacher collected in the books, pencils and rulers and told the class to go.

4. The computer broke and had to be taken to the shop for repair.

5. Don't forget to bring the briefcase, the bag and the umbrella.

6. Jenny carried a heavy suitcase to the taxi. She was going to the airport.

7. The lorry was stuck in a traffic-jam. The driver hoped he would be able to make his delivery before the shop closed.

8. At nursery school, Liam drew a picture, wrote a story, sang a song and listened to his favourite story.

9. Jade got a jigsaw, a book, some crayons and a special doll for Christmas.

10. Lee had worked in a grocer's shop, a factory, a garage, a cinema and now he was working in a hospital.

Exercise Two:

Here are the meanings of ten *common nouns* which all begin with the letter *m*. A dictionary and Thesaurus may help you. Write the word on the line provided.

1. You might use this type of road to travel quickly by car_____

2. A place where people may gather to buy and sell provisions_____

3. A covering for all or part of your face, often worn as disguise_____

4. A type of squirrel which burrows _____

5. A person who builds with stone_____

6. A piece of steel which has the property of attracting iron _____

7. A body of citizen soldiers called upon in an emergency only _____

8. A civil officer administering the law in a court _____

9. A waterproof coat or cloak _____

10. A sweet, musical arrangement of words _____

THE PROPER NOUN

Proper nouns are the title or *names* of specific things: places, people or things.

Example:

PEOPLE	PLACES	THINGS
James	**London**	**Windsor Castle**
Brian	**Paris**	**The Planetarium**
Sara	**America**	**Atlantic Ocean**
Winston Churchill	**India**	**The Alps**

All proper nouns begin with a capital letter.

PRACTICE : THE PROPER NOUN

Exercise Three: _____

Underline and give a capital letter to each of the *proper nouns* in the following sentences.

1. london and paris are capital cities.

2. Our school presented the musical, 'grease', last year. It was a great success thanks to all the hard work put in by miss carpenter.

3. The captain of the football team, barry brocklehurst, has called a practice for next tuesday. Can james come?

4. We went to the grand canyon in america for our holidays last year.

5. susy's heart missed a beat as zak put down his guitar and came towards her.

6. sara and jessica went to see mrs doubtful at the local cinema last Monday.

7. brian, jenny and shaun are all going to swim at the oasis leisure centre this afternoon in hunstable. Can dale come too?

8. What are you wearing to nicky's party on new year's eve?

9. charley, harry and barnaby are just three of thomasina's kittens.

10. Have you heard the latest releases of michael jackson and wet, wet, wet?

Exercise Four: _____

Below are the clues of ten *proper nouns* which are the names of cities, rivers, oceans, canals, countries and mountain ranges which all begin with the letter *P*. Can you discover what they are and write the word on the line provided? You may need an Atlas to help you.

1. The capital city of America is on this river _____

2. A range of hills forming the 'backbone' of England _____

3. The largest ocean in the world _____

4. The range of mountains separating France from Spain _____

5. The capital city of France _____

6. A country in South America _____

7. Pittsburg is in this American state _____

8. The largest canal in Central America _____

9. Manila is found in these Islands in the Pacific Ocean _____

10. Warsaw is the capital city of this country _____

COLLECTIVE NOUNS

Words which tell us the *names* of groups or collections are called collective nouns.

Example:
We say: a *team* of footballers
              a *bunch* of grapes
              a *forest* of trees
              a *school* of whales

PRACTICE : COLLECTIVE NOUNS

Exercise Five: _____

Fill in the following *collective nouns* on the line provided. A dictionary may help.

1. A _____ of lions.   8. A _____ of birds.

2. A _____ of monkeys.   9. A _____ of ships.

3. A _____ of singers.   10. A _____ of soldiers.

4. A _____ of cows.   11. A _____ of wolves.

5. A _____ of bees.   12. A _____ of books.

6. A _____ of flowers.   13. A _____ of geese.

7. A _____ of whales.   14. A _____ of fish.

Can you find the *collective noun* which belongs to each of these groups? They may be more difficult to find and a dictionary may be necessary. The first letter of the *collective noun* is given.

1. A s_____ of clouds.   3. A k_____ of kittens.

2. A c_____ of cats.   4. A c_____ of choughs.

THE ABSTRACT NOUN

An abstract noun stands for a thing which is not material, solid or concrete. These things exist, but you cannot see, touch, taste, smell or hear them.

An abstract noun may be:
A. Something *experienced with your emotions or feelings.*
Example:

pain   pity   grief   sorrow   joy   love
    anger   dismay   sympathy   desire   happiness

B. Something you *know or understand with your mind.*
Example:

science   maths   art   religion

C. The *state or condition* of a person or thing.
Example:

danger   life   peace   poverty   childhood   adulthood

D. A *quality* of a person or thing.
Example:

height   hardness   colour   justice
    force   success   stupidity   ability

E. The *name of an action*.
Example:

| discussion | decision | growth | reduction | addition |
| arrangement | measurement | organization | laughter | revenge |

(See *Grammar Rules and Practice 2 –The Verb*)

The spelling of abstract nouns:
The most common endings are *ness*, *ment*, *ship*, *hood*, *dom*, *ty*, *cy*, *ence* and *ance*.
(See *Spelling Rules and Practice 6* in this series of books for more details and Practice Exercises.)

PRACTICE : THE ABSTRACT NOUN

An abstract noun cannot be touched or felt.
It denotes a quality, condition or emotion.

Exercise Six:_____

Below are listed thirty abstract nouns. There are six of each of the types listed in the notes above. Sort them into the correct category A to E.

law	stickiness	colour	medicine
size	manhood	concern	meeting
innocence	poverty	speed	hardness
guilt	religion	love	grief
spite	fight	discussion	history
voyage	motherhood	hate	softness
childhood	decision	geography	battle
science			anger

SINGULAR AND PLURAL NOUNS

When we speak of a noun being in the *singular* we are talking about *one* noun, one thing.
We say that a noun is in the *plural* when we are talking about *more than one* noun, more than one thing.

There are 14 Rules for forming the plural of nouns.

1. To most nouns we simply add *s*.
Example:

one table   two tables

2. Nouns ending in a hissing sound, such as *x*, *z*, *ss*, *ch*, *sh*, we add *es*.
Example:

one church   two churches   one fox   two foxes

3. Nouns ending in *y* which is preceded by a consonant, change the *y* to an *i* and add *es*.
Example:
                one baby   two babies   one lady   two ladies

4. Nouns which end in *y* which is preceded by a vowel, simply add *s*.
Example:
                one toy   two toys   one day   two days

5. Some nouns ending in *f* (or *fe*) change the *f* (or *fe*) to a *v* and add *es*.
Example:
                one calf   two calves   one loaf   two loaves
These nouns include: elf, half, knife, leaf, life, loaf, self, shelf, thief, wife wolf.

6. Some nouns which end in *f*, simply add *s*.
Example:
                one thief   two thiefs   one roof   two roofs
These nouns include: belief, chief, cliff, cuff, puff roof.

7. Some nouns ending in *o*, add *es*.
Example:
                one tomato two tomatoes   one hero   two heroes
These nouns include: echo, hero, potato and tomato.

8. Other nouns ending in *o* (especially those associated with music), simply add *s*.
Example:
                one piano   two pianos   one radio   two radios
These nouns include: cello, photo, piano, radio solo.

9. Some nouns change completely in the plural.
Some change their *vowels*.
Example:
                one man   two men   one goose   two geese
These nouns include: foot/feet, tooth/teeth, goose/geese, woman/women, mouse/mice.

Some add *en*.
Example:
                one ox   two oxen   one child   two children

10. Some nouns have the same form in the singular and the plural.
Example:
                one sheep two sheep   one series two series
These nouns include: aircraft, deer, hovercraft, spacecraft, species, scissors.

11. Some nouns are always in the plural.

Example:

spectacles   scissors

These nouns include: trousers, jeans, pyjamas, shorts, tights.

Note the following nouns which have a plural spelling but are treated as a **singular** noun: news, mathematics, physics, economics, athletics, rabies, billiards and politics. A singular verb should be used with these nouns.
Example:
We say: Mathematics *is* my favourite subject.
not   Mathematics are my favourite subject.

12. Some nouns have two forms of the plural.
Example:

one penny   two pennies or pence   one fish   two fish or fishes

Note: the plural of person is *people*, not persons.

13. To nouns which consist of more than one word, often hyphenated, add *s* to the main word.
Example:
one daughter-in-law   two daughters-in-law   one passer-by   two passers-by

Nouns which consist of more than one word are called **compound nouns**.
Sometimes the two parts of the word are both nouns. These two nouns can be joined together, hyphenated or remain as two separate words.
Example:

toothbrush   football   shoe shop   tin-opener   taxi driver

To form the plural of these nouns add the *s* or *es* to the final part of the word.
The first part of the word always remains in the singular.
Example:

one toothbrush   two toothbrushes   one shoe shop   two shoe shops
one taxi driver   two taxi drivers   one tin-opener   two tin-openers

Exceptions include *compound* nouns which have *clothes*, *sports*, *men* or *women* as part of the word, in which case the first part of the word is also plural.
Example:

one sports shop   two sports shops   one clothes hanger   two clothes hangers

Some compound nouns may be formed by adding:
    a.   the *ing* form of the verb(present participle) to a noun,
    b.   an adjective to a noun.
Example:

one shopping bag   two shopping bags   one waiting room   two waiting rooms
one greenhouse   two greenhouses   one blackboard   two blackboards

In all these cases the first part of the word remains singular and the *s* or *es* is added to the final part of the word.

14. Some nouns borrowed from foreign languages change according to the following Rules:

Example:

Change *us* to *i*:	one cactus	two cacti
Change *is* to *es*:	one crisis	two crises
Change *um* to *a*:	one rostrum	two rostra
Add *x* to *eau*:	one chateau	two chateaux

PRACTICE : SINGULAR AND PLURAL NOUNS

There are 14 Rules for forming the plural:

1. **To most nouns simply add *s*.**
2. **Nouns ending in a hissing sound, such as *x*, *z*, *ss*, *ch*, *sh*, add *es*.**
3. **Nouns ending in *y* which is preceded by a consonant, change the *y* to an *i* and add *es*.**
4. **Nouns which end in *y* which is preceded by a vowel, simply add *s*.**
5. **Some nouns ending in *f* (or *fe*) change the *f* (or *fe*) to a *v* and add *es*.**
6. **Some nouns which end in *f*, simply add *s*.**
7. **Some nouns ending in *o*, add *es*.**
8. **Other nouns ending in *o*, (especially those associated with music) simply add *s*.**
9. **Some nouns change completely in the plural.**
10. **Some nouns have the same form in the singular and the plural.**
11. **Some nouns are always in the plural.**
12. **Some nouns have two forms of the plural.**
13. **To nouns which consist of more than one word (compound nouns) add the *s* to the final or main part of the word.**
    The first part of the word usually remains in the singular.
14. **Some nouns borrowed from foreign languages change according to the following Rules:**
    Change *us* ending to *i*
    Change *is* ending to *es*
    Change *um* ending to *a*
    Add *x* to an *eau* ending

Exercise Seven: _____

Write the plural of the following.

ox	monkey	pony	fox	echo	mouse	deer	cupful	thief	tooth
shelf	crisis	life	gulf	domino	foot	atlas	calf	cargo	radius	trolley
wolf	baby	story	roof	radio	rostrum	gas	aircraft	goose

The spelling of the singular and plural was dealt with very thoroughly in *Spelling Rules and Practice 3*. For more Practice Exercises please refer to that book.

COUNTABLE and UNCOUNTABLE NOUNS

When a noun has a singular and a plural form, we call this a **countable** noun.
We can count a countable noun. Most nouns are countable nouns.

   one bed   two beds   a child   some children

Before countable nouns we use *a, an, some* or a *number*.

Some nouns, which have no plural form, are **uncountable** nouns.
weather rice milk coffee tea read furniture traffic luggage advice information

We do not usually use *a, an* or a *number** in front of an uncountable noun.
We do not say: one weather   two rice   three milk   four work
but we could use *some*:

   some milk   some rice   some tea   some information

* We would use a number in front of tea and coffee if we were ordering these in a
restaurant. We could say, "Three teas, please."
Some nouns can be used as a countable and an uncountable noun. In these cases we
are usually meaning something different when we use the same word.

Example:

   three glasses of water   he bought some glass from the glazier
   a hair on your jacket   she has blond hair
   iron my shirts   the girder was made of iron

PRACTICE : COUNTABLE AND UNCOUNTABLE NOUNS

> **Nouns which have a singular and a plural form are countable nouns.**
> **We can *count* a countable noun.**
> **Before countable nouns we use *a, an, some* or a *number*.**
>
> **Uncountable nouns have no plural form.**
> **We cannot use *a, an* or a *number* in front of an uncountable noun**
> **but we can use *some*.**
> **Some nouns can be used as a countable and an uncountable noun.**
> **In these cases we are usually meaning something different when we**
> **use the same word.**

Exercise Eight:_____

Identify which ten nouns of the following are *countable* and which ten nouns are *uncountable*. List them under the correct heading.

apple	meat	water	cheese
advice	egg	rice	furniture
luggage	work	book	traffic
handbag	bread	pamphlet	information
paper	desk	carrot	orange

THE DEFINITE AND INDEFINITE ARTICLE

When we are being specific about a noun, we use the definite article, *the*, in front of the noun.

When we are being non-specific about a noun, we use the indefinite article, *a* or *an* in front of the noun. When do we use *a* and when do we use *an*?

1. Use *a* in front of a word which begins with a consonant (except *silent h*).
Example:

> a teacher
> a student
> a building
> a table

2. Use *a* in front of a word which begins with a vowel which sounds like a consonant.
Example:

> a union (u sounds y as in you)
> a one (o sounds w as in won)

3. Use *an* in front of a word which begins with a vowel: *a, e, i, o* and *u*.
Example:

> an office
> an apple
> an increase

4. Use *an* in front of a word which begins with a *silent h*.
Example:

> an honour
> an hour
> an heir

The plural from of the definite article, *the*, remains the same, *the*.

> *The* programmes are already on *the* chairs in the main hall.

The plural from of the infinite article, *a*, is *some*. This changes to *any* when the sentence is in the negative.

There are *some* apples in the dish but there aren't *any* oranges.

PRACTICE : THE DEFINITE AND INDEFINITE ARTICLE

> **Use the definite article, *the*, in front of a singular or plural noun. (specific). Use the indefinite article, *a* or *an* in front of a singular noun, and *some* in front of a plural noun. (non-specific).**
>
> **Use *a* in front of a word which begins with:**
> **1. a consonant (except *silent h*).**
> **2. a vowel which sounds like a consonant.**
>
> **Use *an* in front of a word which begins with**
> **3. a vowel: *a, e, i, o* and *u*.**
> **4. a *silent h*.**

Exercise Nine: _____

There are twenty words below. Ten are preceded with the indefinite article *a*, and ten with *an*. Place the words into the correct columns: words preceded by *a*, and words preceded by *an*.

heir	unicorn	song	orange
onion	hoop	umbrella	unit
hospital	university	envelope	examination
ice-cream	husband	engineer	hamburger
operator	hour	house	union

GENDER

Nouns and pronouns belong to one of four possible *genders* in grammar.
The four genders are:
1. **Masculine**: for words which denote *male* creatures: *boy, prince, waiter*.
2. **Feminine**: for words which denote *female* creatures: *girl, queen, actress*.
3. **Common**: for words denoting creatures of *either sex*.
The same word can be used for both the male and the female: *child, audience, owner*.
4. **Neuter**: for words denoting things of *neither sex* such as *table, lamp, house, computer*. These words denote non-living, inanimate objects.

PRACTICE : GENDER

There are four genders in English Grammar:
> 1. Masculine
> 2. Feminine
> 3. Common
> 4. Neuter

Exercise Ten: _____

Underline the 15 nouns below which are common in gender, cross out the 11 nouns which are neuter in gender, loop in red the 7 nouns which are feminine in gender and in blue, the 7 nouns which are masculine in gender.

sausage	passenger	actor	waitress
audience	table	hero	book
glass	hostess	cup	swimmer
earl	paper	fowl	people
pedestrian	queen	child	girl
window	bachelor	librarian	bed
solicitor	house	lord	mother
priest	passer-by	curtain	reader
cat	bride	journalist	wife
owner	choir	plate	nephew

FAMILIES

Exercise Eleven: _____

These Exercises are referring to the specific names given to the members of a family.
A sheep (common gender) could be a ram (masculine) or a ewe (feminine) or a young animal, a lamb (common gender). Complete the chart with the correct family name.
Choose from these:

Male	Female	Young animal
_____	ewe	_____
stallion	_____	_____
_____	lioness	_____
_____	duck	_____
_____	_____	chicken
_____	cow	_____
_____	goose	_____
boar	_____	_____
_____	_____	leveret
_____	nanny goat	_____
_____	_____	pup

THE ADJECTIVE

An adjective is a describing word.
It describes, or *qualifies*, a noun or pronoun.

Adjectives are words which describe (or qualify) people, places and things (nouns and pronouns). They tell us more about them.

Used thoughtfully, they add meaning to characters, places, events and moods. There is an endless variety of adjectives in the English vocabulary, and when writing an essay you should always try to use adjectives to more fully describe the person, place or thing (noun) you are talking about. A Thesaurus is a good source of adjectives. Use a Thesaurus to find a more appropriate or interesting adjective than perhaps the first adjective that springs to mind.

Example:
Instead of describing a story as *interesting*, you could say the story was:
exciting, gripping, sensational, stimulating, shocking, amusing, unusual, original

Instead of *boring*, you might describe a story as:
tiresome, tedious, unvaried, dreary, drab, commonplace, ponderous, pedestrian, humourless, unexciting, uninteresting, monotonous

Make your writing *sensational!* Don't be dull, be interesting and use adjectives to create the best effect in your writing.

Some detail about adjectives

a. There is only one spelling of an adjective. It does not matter whether it is used to describe a noun in the singular or in the plural there is only one spelling.
Example:
The *rowdy* child... The *rowdy* children... The *brave* soldier... The *brave* soldiers...

b. The spelling of an adjective is always in the singular. This is true even when a *noun* is used as an adjective.
Example:
The children are on holiday for two (adj.) weeks (noun).
The two-week (adjective) courses are fully booked.

There are only two positions in the sentence for an adjective.
c. Most adjectives precede the noun they describe.
Example:
The *white* clouds scudded across the *blue* sky.

BUT:

d. The noun and the adjective may be separated by some verbs such as:
to be, to look, to seem, to appear, to feel, to taste, to smell and to sound
Example:

The *angry* boy...	The boy **looked** *angry*.
The *delicious* meat...	The meat **tasted** *delicious*.
The *anxious* lady...	The lady **seemed** *anxious*.

e. There are some adjectives which are never found next to the noun they describe.
These adjectives include:

    ill   well   awake   asleep   alive   afraid   alone
Example:

The man is *awake*.	never	The *awake* man...
The child was *afraid* of the dark.	never	The *afraid* child...
The lady is looking very *well*.	never	The *well* lady...

Except that they change their form:

asleep becomes *sleeping*	*afraid* becomes *frightened*
ill becomes *sick*	*well* becomes *healthy,* and so on.

Example:

The man is *asleep*.	The *sleeping* man snored.
The baby is *well*.	The *healthy* baby was taken for a walk.
The child is *afraid*.	The *frightened* child could not sleep.
The plant is *alive*.	The *living* plant had pink flowers.

f. An adjective of measurement usually follows the measurement noun.
Example:
If *years* is the *measurement noun* and *old* is the *adjective*:
He is twelve **years** *old* on Tuesday.
If *metres* is the *measurement noun* and *tall* is the *adjective*:
She is 1.35 **metres** *tall*.

g. When there is more than one adjective describing the same noun, an adjective of *opinion* usually precedes an adjective of *fact*.
Example:
A *pretty, slim* girl got off the bus.
A comma would separate these adjectives to avoid reading this as *pretty slim...*
I have just read an *interesting, science-fiction* novel by Arthur C. Clarke.
She was wearing a *beautiful, blue* dress.

In each case, the adjective which expresses your *opinion* precedes the adjective of *fact*.

It is your *opinion* that each noun above is *pretty* or *interesting* or *beautiful*.
It is a *fact* that she is, or is not slim; the dress is, or is not blue; the novel is or is not a science-fiction novel.

h. Finally where there are two or more adjectives of *fact* describing the same noun, they usually come in this order:

> **size, age, shape, colour, origin, material and purpose then the noun.**
> S   A   S   C   O   M   P
> Sara and Sally climbed over the metal post

Example:

> The *small, round, blue, rubber* ball bounced over the hedge and into the road.
>
> (size, shape, colour, material)
>
> The *old, metal, roasting* tray was too small for the chicken.
>
> (age, material, purpose)

HOW AN ADJECTIVE IS FORMED

It was said at the beginning of this book:

The position of a word in the sentence and its consequent relationship with the other words in the sentence, determines the function of that word and hence its part of speech.

It follows therefore, that since most adjectives come immediately in front of the noun they describe, **then any noun or verb placed in front of a noun or pronoun which it describes, must act as an adjective.**

Example:

> There is a church in the middle of the *village*.(noun)
> *Village* shops sell everything from newspapers to tins of paint.(adjective)

Note here that when the noun *shops* is plural, the noun acting as an adjective *village* remains singular. This is in accordance with point b above

> We went for a drive in the *country*.(noun)
> The children liked to visit the *country* park to see the animals.(adjective)
> The man was *driving* his car fast.(verb)
> The *driving* rain beat against the house.(adjective)

Many adjectives are formed from nouns, particularly abstract nouns. Usually the spelling of the ending of the noun is altered to form an adjective. (See *Spelling Rules and Practice 6* in this series of books for more details and further Practice Exercises.)

Example:

1. By adding *ful* to an abstract noun an adjective is formed:

> care *careful*,   beauty *beautiful*,   hate *hateful*,   spite *spiteful*

When *full* stands alone, it has 2 *ll*s. When it is added as a suffix to another word, usually an abstract noun, it loses one of its *l*s and becomes *ful*.

2. By adding *ic* to a noun:		3. By adding *ous* to a noun:		4. By adding *ish*, *al*, *en* and *y*:	
hero	*heroic*	danger	*dangerous*	fool	*foolish*
metal	*metallic*	courage	*courageous*	loyalty	*loyal*
energy	*energetic*	grief	*grievous*	gold	*golden*
electricity	*electric*	anxiety	*anxious*	noise	*noisy*

Some Proper adjectives formed from proper nouns also end in *ish*.

Britain British,   Ireland Irish,   Scotland Scottish,   England English

Adjectives formed from common nouns include:

fool foolish,   baby babyish,   child childish,   self selfish,   bull bullish

5. Adjectives referring to the points of the compass end in *ern*:

north   northern,   south   southern,   west   western,   east   eastern

PRACTICE : ADJECTIVES

> **a. There is only one spelling of an adjective.**
> **b. The spelling of an adjective is always in the singular.**
> **c. Most adjectives precede the noun they describe.**
> **d. Except that they change their form, a noun and an adjective may be separated by some verbs.**
> **e. An adjective of measurement usually follows the measurement noun.**
> **f. When there is more than one adjective describing the same noun, an adjective of *opinion* usually precedes an adjective of *fact*.**
> **g. Where there are two or more adjectives of *fact* describing the same noun, they precede the noun in this order: size, age, shape, colour, origin, material, purpose.**
> **Many adjectives are formed from nouns.**

Exercise Twelve: _____

Change the following nouns into adjectives by adding an appropriate ending. Choose from *ful, ic, ous* and *y*. Test the accuracy of your choice by mentally placing each adjective you create in front of a noun to see if it describes it.

care	centre	spite	athlete	metal
courage	giant	hero	winter	might
beauty	base	hate	luxury	peril
industry	grief	electricity	fault	shadow
autumn	voice	noise	anxiety	hope

TYPES OF ADJECTIVE

There are three types of adjective:

        1. Adjectives of Quality
        2. Adjectives of Quantity
        3. Adjectives of Distinction

1. Adjectives of Quality
Adjectives of quality simply describe a noun or pronoun. They are descriptive adjectives. They answer the question *what kind of?*
Example:

>The *loud* music angered the *impatient* man.

Ask:

What kind of music?	Answer: loud	*Loud* is therefore an *adjective of quality*.
What kind of man?	Answer: impatient	*Impatient* is an *adjective of quality*.

Other Adjectives of quality include:
fierce, brave, bright, clean, dark, cruel, curved, happy, keen, clean, old, young, angry.

2. Adjectives of Quantity
Adjectives of quantity indicate number or amount.
An adjective of quantity answers the question *how many?* or *how much?*
Example: much, more, most, little.
Sometimes this amount is a vague quantity (sometimes referred to as *indefinite*), sometimes it is a precise (*definite*) quantity.
A number is a noun, but when used to describe another noun or pronoun it acts as an adjective. A number which tells the order (first, second, third) can also be a noun or an adjective.
Example:

>*Ten* girls in the class managed to answer *all* the questions.

Ask:

How many girls?   Answer: *ten*   *Ten* is therefore an *adjective of quantity* (definite).
How many questions? Answer: *all*   *All* is therefore an *adjective of quantity* (indefinite).

3. Adjectives of Distinction
These distinguish or *set apart* one noun from another noun of the same kind.
There are four kinds of adjective which distinguish.

A. Demonstrative Adjectives
These answer the question *which?* or *what?*
Example:

>*This* pencil should be placed in *that* drawer over there.

Ask:

Which pencil?	Answer: *This* pencil.	*This* is a demonstrative adjective.
Which drawer?	Answer: *That* drawer.	*That* is a demonstrative adjective.

Both *this* and *that* are distinguishing, *demonstrating* which particular noun we are talking about.

>*Which* pencil? *This* pencil (here), not that pencil (over there).
>*Which* drawer? *That* drawer (over there), no other.

They are both adjectives because they are placed next to the noun which they are distinguishing or *demonstrating*.
(We shall compare demonstrative adjectives with demonstrative pronouns later.)

This refers to something *close by* (here). *These* is the *plural* of this.
That refers to something which is *not close by* (over there). *Those* is its *plural*.
The definite(*the*) and indefinite articles(*a* and *an*) may also be considered
demonstrative adjectives.
Example:

Pass me *the* book and place it on *that* desk.
Which book? Answer: *the* book. (Not just any book, but *the* book.)
Which table?Answer: *that* table. (Not just any table, but *that* table.)

The and *that* are both demonstrative adjectives which point out *which* book and *which*
table we are talking about.

B. Possessive Adjectives

These answer the question *Whose?*
Example:

This is *my* pencil, that is *his* book and over there is *her* bag.

Ask:

Whose pencil?	Answer: *my pencil.*
Whose book?	Answer: *his* book.
Whose bag?	Answer: *her* bag.

My, *his* and *her* are possessive adjectives answering the question *whose* pencil, *whose*
book, *whose* bag?

A *possessive adjective* is always next, or near to, the noun it describes or qualifies. The
noun is **always** present. In this respect, it differs from a possessive pronoun which
takes the place of the noun. (Possessive Pronouns will be looked at in the next section.)

**If there is a noun present, it is a possessive adjective. If there is no noun, it is
a possessive pronoun. Take care!**

C. Interrogative Adjectives

An *interrogative* asks a question; it requires a question mark.
An *interrogative adjective* asks:

Which?   *What?*   *Whose?*

Example:

Which book is on the table?
What colour is her dress?
Whose trainers are these?

**Each *interrogative adjective* is placed in front of the noun or pronoun it
qualifies.**

In this respect they differ from an interrogative pronoun which is not followed by a
noun or pronoun. We shall look at interrogative pronouns in the next section.

It can be seen, then, that *adjectives of distinction* distinguish one noun from another
noun of the same kind.
They do this by asking:

Which?   *What?*   *Whose?*

Each question is answered by an *adjective of distinction*:
This   That   These   Those   My   Your   His   Her   Its   Our   Their

Each of these is an adjective only when it has a noun or pronoun nearby which it qualifies. If there is no noun or pronoun nearby, it is not an adjective, it is a pronoun. Take care!
This is discussed fully in the next section.

D. Finally, there are Distributive Adjectives
Distributive adjectives refer separately to individual people or items in a group.
Distributive adjectives include: *each*, *every*, *either* and *neither*.
Example:

He could travel home by *either* route.
Every child has ambition.
Each day is special.

PRACTICE : TYPES OF ADJECTIVE

> There are three types of adjective:
>
> **1. Adjectives of Quality**
> **2. Adjectives of Quantity**
> **3. Adjectives of Distinction**

> 1. **Adjectives of Quality** *describe* **a noun or pronoun.**
>   **They answer the question** *what kind of?*
> 2. **Adjectives of Quantity indicate** *number* **or** *amount*.
>   **They answer the question** *how many?* **or** *how much?*
> 3. **Adjectives of Distinction** *set apart* **one noun from another**
>   **noun of the same kind.**
>   **There are four kinds of adjective which distinguish:**
>   **A. Demonstrative Adjectives.**
>   **These answer the question** *which?* **or** *what?*
>   **B. Possessive Adjectives.**
>   **These answer the question** *Whose?*
>   **C. Interrogative Adjectives ask a question.**
>   **These ask:** *Which? What? Whose?*
>   **D. Distributive Adjectives refer separately to the individual**
>   **people or items in a group.**

Exercise Thirteen: _____

Identify which type of adjective is being used in the following sentence. The adjectives are italicised.

1. *Most* girls in my class have *some* magazines at home.
2. *That* book over there is *my* book.
3. *Whose* car is parked in front of *that* locked gate?
4. *Every* person I ask has an *interesting* hobby.
5. *Six* families in our street have *blue* cars.
6. *What* present would you like for Christmas?
7. *Children's* toys must be safe.
8. *Several* girls I know are in *that* play.
9. *These* apples taste better than *those* apples.
10. *Most young* men spend *their* money at the weekend.

THE COMPARISON OF ADJECTIVES

An *adjective* is a word that modifies or qualifies a noun or pronoun.
An *adverb*, which will be studied in detail in *Grammar Rules and Practice 2*, is a word that modifies a verb, an adjective, or another adverb.
Both adjectives and adverbs are found in one of three forms of *comparative degree.*

There are three *degrees of comparison: positive, comparative* and *superlative.*
1. The *positive* degree is simply descriptive, used when expressing simple quality of **one** noun on its own without comparison.
Example:

> The *tall* building (positive degree)
> The *loud* voice

2. We use the *comparative* degree of an adjective (or adverb) to express a higher degree of a quality. We use the *comparative degree* when we are comparing **two** nouns. We say:

> This building is *tall* (positive degree)
> but   that building is *taller* (comparative degree).
> His voice is *loud*
> but   her voice is *louder.*

3. The *superlative* degree of a one syllable adjective (or adverb) ends in *est* and is used to express the highest degree of a quality and is used when **more than two** nouns are compared.
Example:

> This building is tall (positive degree)
> but   that building is tall*er* (comparative degree).
> Of all the buildings I know, that building is the tall*est* (superlative degree).

The *comparative degree* of an adjective or an adverb of one syllable ends in *er* and the *superlative degree* ends in *est*. A word of MORE than two syllables

does not end in *er* **or** *est,* **but is preceded by the word** *more* **in the** *comparative* **degree and** *most* **in the** *superlative* **degree.**
Example:
Adjective:

	This lady is *beautiful*	(positive degree)
	that lady is *more beautiful*	(comparative degree)
but	that lady is *most beautiful*	(superlative degree)

Make a particular note of the irregular adjectives which have quite different forms in the *comparative* and *superlative* degree.

These irregular adjectives include:

good better best	little less least
bad worse worst	many more most
far farther farthest	much more most

Irregular adverbs are discussed in The Adverb *Grammar Rules and Practice 2.*

THE USES OF COMPARATIVES

We use comparatives when we are comparing one person or thing with another.
a. After a comparative we often use *than.*
Example:

> The Amazon is longer than...
> Good health is more important than...

b. *A comparative + a comparative* **are often put together.**
Example:

> The sun is getting hotter and hotter...

c. To say that two things change together or that one thing depends on another, we use *the + comparative clause, the + comparative clause.*
Example:

> The *larger* the car the *harder* it is to find a parking space.

d. Words such as *very, much, a lot, a little, rather* **and** *far* **can be used before a comparative.**
Example:

> He is *a lot* taller than I thought.
> It is *rather* hotter than I anticipated.
> It is *far* colder today than before.

USE OF THE SUPERLATIVE

The superlative is used to compare one thing or person in a group with two or more other persons or things in the same group.
Example:

> Sara is tall, Liam is taller but James is the tallest of the children.

a. Often, *the* is used with the superlative.
Example:

> Jade is *the* cleverest person in her class.
> Charley is *the* naughtiest kitten I know.
> Jenny is *the* busiest person I've met.

b. *By far* and *easily* is also used before the superlative.
Example:

> She is *by far* the tallest person in her school.
> This book is *easily* the most interesting book I have ever read.

PRACTICE : THE COMPARISON OF ADJECTIVES

There are three *degrees of comparison*:
1. **The *positive* degree** involves **one** noun without comparison.
2. **The *comparative* degree** compares **two** nouns.
3. **The *superlative* degree** is used when **more than two** nouns are compared.

Adjectives of one syllable:
> The *comparative degree* ends in *er*.
> The *superlative degree* ends in *est*.

Adjectives of MORE than one syllable:
> The *comparative* degree is preceded by the word *more*.
> The *superlative* degree is preceded by the word *most*.

There are some irregular adjectives.

Usage:
> a. After a comparative we often use *than*.
> b. *A comparative* and *a comparative* are often
>   put together.
> c. When two things change together or one thing
>   depends on another,
use *the + comparative clause, the + comparative clause*.
> d. *very, much, a lot, a little, rather* and *far* can be used
>   before a comparative.

The superlative:
> a. Often, *the* is used with the superlative.
> b. *By far* and *easily* is also used before the superlative.

Exercise Fourteen: _____

Below is given the *positive degree* of 20 adjectives. Fill in the *comparative* and *superlative* degrees in the spaces provided. Remember to add *er* to a one-syllable word in the comparative degree and *est* in the superlative degree. To words of more than one syllable add *more* to form the comparative degree and *most* to form the superlative degree.

Positive	Comparative	Superlative
bad	_____	_____
beautiful	_____	_____
slow	_____	_____
high	_____	_____
cheeky	_____	_____
good	_____	_____
happy	_____	_____
healthy	_____	_____
exciting	_____	_____
long	_____	_____
brown	_____	_____
quick	_____	_____
many	_____	_____
blue	_____	_____
wonderful	_____	_____
calm	_____	_____
patient	_____	_____
little	_____	_____
considerate	_____	_____
slow	_____	_____

(See *Spelling Rules and Practice 3* for more practice exercises.)

THE PRONOUN

A pronoun is a word which takes the place of a noun once the noun, (the thing, place or person) has been mentioned in the sentence (or in the context). *Pro* **means** *acting as a substitute for* **and that is precisely what a pronoun does. A** *pro* **noun acts as a substitute for a noun but only after it is clear** *who* **or** *what* **we are talking about. A pronoun is used to avoid repeating a noun.**
Example:

The *boy* and *girl* left the classroom. *They* had left their books behind.

In the first sentence, *boy* and *girl* are both common nouns. It is very important, that *boy* and *girl* are mentioned in the first sentence so we know exactly who we are talking about. In the second sentence the pronoun *they* can be substituted to avoid repeating *boy* and *girl*. This makes it easier, less jerky and more interesting to read.

There are seven types of pronoun.

1. **The Personal Pronoun**
2. **The Possessive Pronoun**
3. **The Reflexive Pronoun**
4. **The Relative pronoun**
5. **The Interrogative Pronoun**
6. **The Demonstrative Pronoun**
7. **The Indefinite Pronoun**

1. The Personal Pronoun
We use a personal pronoun to replace a noun when it is clear *who* or *what* we are talking about.

When the personal pronoun is **the subject of the sentence** , we use:
I, you, he, she, it   in the singular
we, you, and they   in the plural

When the personal pronoun is **the object of the sentence**, we use:
me, you, him, her, it   in the singular
us, you, and them   in the plural
Example:
Used as the *subject* of the sentence:
Where is Margaret? **She's** in the library.
Lee went to the cinema last night. **He** was home quite late.

Used as the *object* of the sentence:
Charles is a new boy in my class. I like **him** very much.

Here, the object pronoun follows the verb.
Jane sent me a letter from America. I have already written to **her**.
Here, the object pronoun follows the preposition, *to*.

In all these examples, it is clear *who* we are talking about before a pronoun is substituted.

In comparisons, we use object pronouns after *than* or *as*.
Example:
He is tall, but he's not as tall *as **me**.*
We are both thirteen but I'm two months older *than **him**.*

It is also acceptable to use a *subject* pronoun here with the verb and say:
...but I'm two months older than **he is**.
However, this would only be adopted in a very formal style.

Use object pronouns after the verb *to be*.

Example:

Who's there? It's ***me.***

I didn't do it. It was ***him.***

It would be acceptable here, as in the previous example, to use a subject pronoun combined with the verb:

Who's there? It ***is I.***

Though correct, this combination is formal.

We use an object pronoun when the pronoun stands alone in the answer.
Example:

Who's there? ***Me.***   (not I).

The Use of Personal Pronouns

For the person or persons *actually speaking*:
Use *I* or *me*, in the first person singular,
and *we* or *us* in the plural.

For the person or persons *being spoken to*:
Use *you* in the singular and plural.

For a person or animal *being spoken about*:
Use *he* or *him* for the male gender,
she or *her* for the female gender
and *it* for an animal where the gender is not known or is unimportant.
They or *them* for people or things, being spoken about, is used in the plural.

It, whilst usually used for an object or animal when the gender is unimportant or not known, can be used for a person when we are asking, or saying who the person is.
Example:

Who is ***it*** at the door? ***It***'s Dorothy.

It is also used in expressions of *time, distance, weather* and *temperature*.
Example:
It's four o'clock.   ***It***'s two kilometers to the next town.   ***It***'s raining. ***It***'s cold.

It can also begin a sentence taking the place of *a subject in the infinitive*, or a clause beginning with the word *that*.
Example:

It is exciting to go up the Eiffel Tower on a windy day.

instead of: *To go up* the Eiffel Tower on a windy day is exciting.

It's a pity that we couldn't go to the dance.

instead of: *That we couldn't go to the dance*, is a pity.

2. The Possessive Pronoun
A Possessive Pronoun shows *ownership*. A Possessive Pronoun, unlike a possessive adjective, is used *without a noun*. It substitutes, or takes the place of a noun, when the noun is understood.

Example:

Whose is that book? It's **mine**.   (*my* book)

I've done my homework, but Caroline hasn't done **hers**.   (*her* homework)

Our pitch is flatter that **yours**.   (*your* pitch)

Your car is cleaner that **ours**.   (*our* car)

mine, hers, yours and ***ours*** are ***possessive pronouns*. They are used *without a noun*. The noun, however, is understood.**

Don't confuse a possessive pronoun – *which takes the place of a noun completely* – with a possessive adjective. A possessive adjective simply describes *who* owns something. *My* (book), *her* (homework), *your* (pitch) and *our* (car) are possessive adjectives. Each has a noun next to it. A possessive adjective is simply telling us *who* owns the noun. This is not the case with a possessive pronoun where **there is no noun present.**

The possessive Pronouns are:

	mine	yours	his	her	in the singular
and	ours	yours	and	theirs	in the plural.

3. Reflexive Pronouns

Reflexive pronouns are used when the subject and the object of the clause or sentence is the same.

Example:

I looked at **myself** in the mirror.

He burnt **himself** when he touched the fire.

They hurt **themselves** when they came off the motorbike.

It is as though the ***reflexive pronoun*** is *looking back*, or *reflecting* on the subject of the clause or sentence.

The **Reflexive Pronouns** are:

myself	yourself	himself	herself	and	itself	in the singular
and	ourselves	yourselves	and	themselves		in the plural.

A **reflexive pronoun** is not usually used with an action a person does to himself, such as, *wash, shave, dress*. We do, however, say he **dried** himself with a towel.

Reflexive pronouns can also be used to *emphasise* what a person did - that *he* did something, and nobody else.

Example:

Nobody helped me decorate the house. I did it all by **myself**.

You have to do the work all by **yourself**.

Reflexive pronouns, used in this way, usually come at the end of the sentence. However, they can immediately follow the subject of the sentence.

Example:

The Queen **herself** opened the conference.

I **myself** am better at tennis than squash.

In both cases, the reflexive pronouns are being used to *emphasise* a person. They are therefore called ***emphatic pronouns.***

PRACTICE 1 : THE PRONOUN

A *pro* noun takes the place of a noun once the noun
has been mentioned in the sentence (or in the context)
and it is clear *who* or *what* we are talking about.
A pronoun is used to avoid repeating a noun.
There are seven types of pronoun.

1.	Personal Pronouns	5.	Interrogative Pronouns
2.	Possessive Pronouns	6.	Demonstrative Pronouns
3.	Reflexive Pronouns	7.	Indefinite Pronouns
4.	Relative pronouns		

1.   A Personal Pronoun is used when it is clear
who or *what* is being talked about.
Use an object pronoun in comparisons after *than* or *as*
and after the verb *to be*.

2.   Possessive Pronouns show *ownership*. They is used *without
a noun.Mine, hers, yours* and *ours* are *possessive pronouns.*

3.   Reflexive Pronouns are used when the subject and the
object of the clause or sentence are the same.
Emphatic Pronouns are reflexive pronouns
which are used to *emphasise.*

Exercise Fifteen: _____

Underline the pronouns in the following sentences and in the brackets at the end of each sentence write
in the code letter to identify the type of pronoun being used. The code letters are: *Ps* for personal
subject, *Po* for personal object, *Pss* for possessive, *R* for reflexive, E for emphatic and D for
demonstrative.

1. I have been looking after myself.
2. I think that book is mine although she says it's hers.
3. He was running along the road towards me.
4. The Queen herself opened the new wing of our school.
5. I baked that cake myself.
6. I have been shopping to buy a present for him.
7. She did better than me in the examinations.
8. "I've been watching you," said the policeman.
9. Her children are too young to look after themselves.
10. Their house is much bigger than ours.

4. The Relative Pronoun

A *relative pronoun* stands in the second part of a sentence for a noun or pronoun in the first part of the sentence. We refer to the noun or pronoun in the first part of the sentence as its *antecedent*. A relative pronoun refers to, and tells us more about the *antecedent*.

Relative pronouns include:

       who   whom   whose   which   that

We use *who* and *whom* for people and *which* for things. *That* can be used for both animals, things and people, singular and plural. *Whose* shows possession.

We use the relative pronouns *who, which* or *that* for the subject of the verb in the relative clause.

Example:

    Sahib, ***who*** is wearing spectacles, asked directions to the hotel.
    The purse, ***which*** was on the table, has been stolen.

Explanation.   <u>For those who need more information.</u>

In the first example, the relative pronoun ***who*** introduces a relative clause (a subordinate clause) which is giving us more information about *Sahib*, its *antecedent*. If we split this example avoiding the use of ***who,*** we would have two sentences:

    Sahib asked directions to the hotel.
    Sahib is wearing spectacles.

To avoid using the name *Sahib* twice, ***who***, a *relative pronoun*, takes the place of Sahib (the antecedent) in the relative clause. Since Sahib (a person) is the **subject of the verb in the relative clause, we use *who.***

Similarly in the second example, the relative pronoun ***which*** introduces a relative clause which is giving us more information about *the purse*, its antecedent. If, like above, we split this sentence into two parts avoiding the use of the word ***which***, we would have two sentences:

    The purse has been stolen.
    The purse was on the table.

To avoid using *the purse* twice, the relative pronoun, ***which***, takes the place of *the purse* (the antecedent) in the relative clause. Since, *the purse* (a thing) is the **subject of the verb in the relative clause, we use *which.***

We can use the relative pronoun *whom* instead of *who* (for people), when it represents the *object* of the verb in the relative clause.

Example:

    John, ***whom*** you have met, is coming for tea.

This sentence really says two things:

    John is coming for tea.
    You have met John.

Here, *John* is the object of the verb in the relative clause. The relative pronoun ***whom*** represents the antecedent *John* (a person), and is the **object of the verb in the relative clause.**

Example:
Did you see the message that your secretary left?
In this example, the relative pronoun that refers to its antecedent *message* which, upon analysis, is the **object** of the relative clause. This sentence is really saying two things:
Did you see the message?
Your secretary left the message.
Message in the second part is the **object** of the verb. ***That*** is a relative pronoun taking the place of the noun *message*. Here, ***that*** fuctions as the object of the relative clause and represents its antecedent, *message*.

We use the relative pronoun *whose* to show possession.
Whose answers the questions:

of whom?	*belonging to whom?*	(*person*, singular or plural)
of which?	*belonging to which?*	(*animal* or *thing*, singular or plural)

In the sentence above:
The lady, whose son swims for the club, has left.
The two things this sentence says are:
The lady has left.
The son of the lady swims for the club.

Who is the owner of the son? The son *of whom, belonging to whom?*
Answer: Of the lady. He is the lady's son.
The relative pronoun ***whose*** represents possession of the antecedent, *lady*.

5. The Interrogative Pronoun
Interrogative pronouns ask questions. They refer to people, animals and things. The interrogative pronouns are: who? which? whom? whose? what?
The choice of interrogative pronoun, like a relative pronoun, depends on the function of the pronoun in the sentence.

Explanation. <u>For those who need more information.</u>
Example:
Who is coming to the party?
Here, ***who*** is really asking:
Which person is coming to the party?
Which person is the subject of the verb. **We use *who* for the subject of the verb when the subject of the verb is *a person*. Who** is an interrogative *pronoun*. **Who** needs no noun, is a substitute for a noun, stands alone as the subject of the verb, and is therefore an **interrogative pronoun.**

By comparison, an interrogative adjective, requires a noun near, or next to it, which it describes or qualifies. *Which* person, for example, is an interrogative adjective because it is followed by the noun *person*. Take care not to confuse interrogative adjectives and pronouns!

Example:
> ***Whom*** do you think I met?

If we rewrite this to determine the function of ***whom,*** we have:
> I met ***which person?*** (do you think?)

Here *which person* is the object of the verb *met*.

The interrogative pronoun which acts as the object of a verb, is *whom*.

6. The Demonstrative Pronoun
Demonstrative pronouns, point out or demonstrate what they stand for.
> This   that   these those

are demonstrative pronouns.

This (singular), these (plural), designate something close by, or most recent in time.

That (singular), those (plural), designate something farther away in time or position.

Example:
> **This** is better than **that.**

Is really saying: This (here) is better than that (there).

A *demonstrative pronoun* stands alone, as the subject or object of the verb, replacing a noun or another pronoun (which is understood) and pointing it out. It differs from a demonstrative adjective which needs a noun or pronoun nearby to point out as well as describe.

Example:
> *This* book is exciting.

Here, *this* is a demonstrative adjective which describes and points out the noun, *book*. It differs from:
> ***This*** is intolerable.

This, demonstrative pronoun, stands alone as the subject of the sentence, representing a noun or pronoun (which is understood) and which it points out.

Example:
> ***This*** is bigger than ***that***

This and *that* are both *demonstrative pronouns* representing and pointing out nouns or pronouns which are understood. These differ from:
> *This house* is bigger than *that house*.

Here, *this* and *that* are demonstrative adjectives pointing out, as well as describing the noun, *house*.

7. The Indefinite Pronoun
Indefinite pronouns take the place of a person, thing or place unspecified.
Example:
> Tell me *more.*
> *Either* will do.
> *Both* came.
> You don't seem to know *much.*

Two common mistakes when using indefinite pronouns:

1. **Do not** refer to a singular *indefinite pronoun* as if it were a plural.

Example:

> Everyone must play *their* part. (wrong)
> Everyone must play *his* part. (correct)

Here, *everyone* is singular, so *his*, singular, is correct; *their*, plural is incorrect.

2. **Do not**, when using the *indefinite pronoun, one*, switch from using *one* to using another pronoun such as *he* or *she*.

Example:

> *One* must use *his* intelligence. (wrong)
> *One* must use *one's* intelligence. (correct)

PRACTICE 2 : THE PRONOUN

> **4. A Relative Pronoun stands in the second part of a sentence.**
> **It refers to, and tells us more about the *antecedent*.**
> **5. Interrogative Pronouns *ask questions*.**
> **6. Demonstrative Pronouns point out or *demonstrate* what they stand for.**
> **7. Indefinite Pronouns take the place of a person, thing or place**
> ***unspecified.***

Exercise Sixteen: _____

Do the same as you did in the previous exercise. This time, in addition to Ps, Po, Pss and R for the first four types of Pronoun we have already practised, use the code *A* for a relative pronoun, *I* for an interrogative, *D* for a demonstrative, *Id* for an indefinite pronoun and E for emphatic. Underline each pronoun and using the code, identify which type of pronoun is being used.

1.   The bag which was on the table was taken by you.
2.   I myself saw you take the purse.
3.   Which is mine? I like that best.
4.   Sara, whom you have met, is coming.
5.   This is better than that. Which do you prefer?
6.   The man who lives next door, is digging his garden.
7.   Both came, but I like him better.
8.   Who is coming to my party?
9.   She is better at English than me.
10. The girl who sits next to me in class is my best friend.

RULE SUMMARIES

Here you are asked to do three things:

1. Read through all the Rules that have been identified in this book, one at a time.
2. When you are ready, fill in the missing words in the Rule Summaries below.
3. Explain in your own words what is meant by each Rule, making references to the examples given.

THE SENTENCE

Read Pages 1 to 5 about **THE SENTENCE** and when you are ready complete the following Rule Summary without referring to those pages.

A sentence is a group of words which begins with a _____ _____ and ends with a ____ ____, _____ or question mark. It makes complete _____ by itself and can stand _____. It usually has a _____ and a predicate with a _____ verb.

A clause has a _____ verb and is either a part of a sentence (_____, subordinate and _____ clauses) or can stand alone and act as a sentence in its own right and make complete sense (_____ clause). A subordinate clause can do the work of an _____, _____ or _____.

A phrase can _____ stand alone as a sentence and must be joined to other words to be given _____. It does not contain a _____. It can act as a _____, adjective or _____.

Now turn back to pages 5 and 6 to check your answer.

KEEPING YOUR OWN RECORD OF THE GRAMMAR RULES IN THESE BOOKS

To keep a permanent record of the Grammar Rules in these books - a record to which you can refer at any time - you need a pack of 5ins x 8ins index cards and an index card box or A5 file.

CARD ONE:

Copy the Rule Summary concerning **THE SENTENCE** from pages 5 and 6 carefully and clearly onto the first side of Card One. Spread out your writing so it is neat and easy to read.

On the reverse of Card One:
1. Explain what is meant by a *simple* and a *complex sentence* (read page 3).
2. Explain what is meant by a *main clause*, a *subordinate clause* and what the difference is between them - that one could stand as a sentence in its own right - which one? The other can do the work of an adjective, adverb etc.
3. What is a *compound sentence*? (Read page 4.)
4. What is a *co-ordinating clause* and how are co-ordinating clauses joined together?
5. What is a *phrase*? (Read page 5.)

In all cases, give as many examples as you feel are necessary to illustrate and clarify your own notes.

CARD TWO:

Copy onto the first side of Card Two the eight parts of speech as listed on page 6.

On the reverse of Card Two:
1. Give an example of each part of speech.
2. Explain in your own words what is meant by a **part of speech** and how a word by changing its position in the sentence can change its function and so its part of speech. Give examples to illustrate your explanation.

CARD THREE:
Read Page 6 about **THE NOUN** and when you are ready complete the following Rule Summary without referring to that page.

A word or group of words (_____ and _____) that tells us the _____ of a
_____, animal, _____ or thing is a *noun*.
There are _____ types of noun:
          1. _____ nouns.   3. _____ nouns.
          2. _____ nouns.   4. _____ nouns.

Now turn back to page 6 to check your answer.

Copy the Rule Summary concerning **THE NOUN** from page 6 carefully and clearly onto the first side of Card Three. Spread out your writing so it is neat and easy to read.

On the reverse of Card Three under each separate heading as listed 1 to 4 above, give four examples of each type of noun.

CARD FOUR:
Read Page 7 about **THE COMMON NOUN** and when you are ready complete the following Rule Summary without referring to that page. if you prefer or if you cannot remember the examples in the text.

Common nouns are the _____ *names* given to different kinds of _____, places,
animals or _____. Common nouns do _____ begin with a _____ letter.

Now turn back to page 7 to check your answer. Copy the Rule Summary concerning **THE COMMON NOUN** from page 7 carefully and clearly onto the first side of Card Four. Spread out your writing so it is neat and easy to read.

On the reverse of Card Four:
1. List examples of your own under the correct headings: people, places, animals and things.
2. Make any additional notes about common nouns which will help you at school.

CARD FIVE:
Read Page 8 about **THE PROPER NOUN** and when you are ready complete the following Rule Summary without referring to that page.

Proper nouns are the title or *names* of _____ things: places, _____ or
_____. All proper nouns begin with a _____ _____.

Now turn back to page 8 to check your answer. Copy the Rule Summary concerning **THE PROPER NOUN** from page 8 carefully and clearly onto the first side of Card Five.

On the reverse of Card Five:
1. 1. List examples of your own under the correct headings: people, places and things.
2. Make any additional notes about proper nouns which will help you at school.

CARD SIX:
Read Page 9 and 10 about **COLLECTIVE NOUNS** and when you are ready complete the following Rule Summary without referring to those pages. Choose examples of your own under the correct heading if you prefer or if you cannot remember the examples in the text.

Words which tell us the *names* of _____ or _____ are called collective nouns.
Example:
We say

      a _____ of footballers   a _____ of whales

      a *bunch* of _____   a _____ of _____

      a _____ of trees   a _____ of _____

Now turn back to page 9 and 10 to check your answer. Copy the Rule Summary concerning **THE COLLECTIVE NOUN** from page 9 carefully and clearly onto the first side of Card Six.

On the reverse of Card Six:
Make any additional notes about collective nouns which will help you at school.

CARD SEVEN:
Read Page 10 and 11 about **ABSTRACT NOUNS** and when you are ready complete the following Rule Summary without referring to those pages. Choose examples of your own under the correct heading if you prefer or if you cannot remember the examples in the text.

An abstract noun stands for a thing which is not _____, solid or _____.
These things exist, but you cannot _____, _____, _____, _____ or hear them.

A. They may be things experienced with your _____ or feelings.
B. Something you _____ or understand with your _____.
C. The state or _____ of a person or thing.
D. A _____ of a person or thing.
E. They may be the names of _____.

Now turn back to pages 10 and 11 to check your answers. Copy the Rule Summary concerning **THE ABSTRACT NOUN** from those pages onto the first side of Card Seven.

On the reverse of Card Seven:
Under the side headings as listed above, A, B, C, D and E, give six examples of each type of abstract noun.

CARD EIGHT:
Read Page 11, 12, 13 and 14 about **SINGULAR AND PLURAL NOUNS** and when you are ready complete the following Rule Summaries without referring to those pages.

There are _____ Rules for forming the plural:
1. To most nouns simply add ___.
2. Nouns ending in a _____ sound, such as __, __, ___, ___, ____, add *es*.
3. Nouns ending in *y* which is preceded by a _____, change the ___ to an ___ and add *es*.
4. Nouns which end in *y* which is preceded by a _____, simply add *s*.
5. Some nouns ending in *f* (or *fe*) change the ___ (or _____) to a ___ and add ____.

6. Some nouns which end in *f*, simply ____ ___.
7. Some nouns ending in *o*, add ____.
8. Other nouns ending in *o*,(especially those associated with _____) simply add *s*.
9. Some nouns _____ _____ in the plural.
10. Some nouns have the same form in the _____ and the _____.
11. Some nouns are always in the _____.
12. Some nouns have two _____ _____ _____ _____.
13. To nouns which consist of more than one word (_____ nouns) add the *s* to the _____ or main part of the word. The first part of the word usually remains in the _____.

14. Some nouns borrowed from foreign languages change according to the following Rules:
Change *us* ending to ___, change ___ ending to *es*, change _____ ending to *a*, add *x* to an _____ ending.

Now turn back to page 14 to check your answer. Copy the Rule Summary concerning **SINGULAR AND PLURAL NOUNS** from page 14 onto the first side of Card Eight.

On the reverse of Card Eight:
Under each separate heading, list three examples to show each spelling of the plural.
Make any additional notes about singular and plural nouns which will help you at school.

CARD NINE:
Read page 15 about **COUNTABLE AND UNCOUNTABLE NOUNS** and when you are ready complete the following Rule Summary without referring to that page.

Nouns which have a singular and a plural form are _____ nouns.We can _____ a countable noun.Before countable nouns we use ___,___, *some* or a _____.

Uncountable nouns have ___ _____ _____. We cannot use *a, an* or a _____ in front of an uncountable noun but we can use _____. Some nouns can be used as a countable and an uncountable noun. In these cases we are usually meaning something _____ when we use the same word.

Now turn back to page 15 to check your answer. Copy the Rule Summary concerning **COUNTABLE AND UNCOUNTABLE NOUNS** from page 15 onto the first side of Card Nine.

On the reverse of Card Nine:
Make additional notes about countable and uncountable nouns that will further explain what is meant by them. Give examples to illustrate your answers.

CARD TEN:
Read Pages 16 and 17 about **THE DEFINITE AND INDEFINITE ARTICLE** and when you are ready complete the following Rule Summary without referring to those pages.

Use the _____ article, *the*, in front of a _____ or plural noun. (_____)
Use the indefinite article, ____ *or* _____ in front of a singular noun, and _____ in front of a plural noun. (non-_____)

Use *a* in front of a word which begins with:
1. a _____ (except _____). 2. a vowel which _____ like a consonant.

Use *an* in front of a word which begins with
3. a _____: *a, e, i,* ____ and ____. 4. a _____ *h.*

Now turn back to page 17 to check your answer. Copy the Rule Summary concerning **THE DEFINITE AND INDEFINITE ARTICLE** from page 17 onto the first side of Card Ten.

On the reverse of Card Ten give examples to illustrate each of the points above.

CARD ELEVEN:
Read Pages 17 and 18 about **GENDER AND FAMILIES** and when you are ready complete the following Rule Summary without referring to those pages.

There are _____ genders in English Grammar:
1. _____ 3. _____ 2. _____ 4. _____

Now turn back to page 18 to check your answer. Copy the Rule Summary concerning **GENDER AND FAMILIES** from page 18 onto the first side of Card Eleven.

On the reverse of Card Eleven give examples to illustrate your answers listing any family members about which you are not sure, for future reference. Refer to the answers of Exercise 11 to help you.

CARD TWELVE:
Read Pages 19 to 22 about **THE ADJECTIVE, SOME DETAIL ABOUT AN ADJECTIVE and HOW AN ADJECTIVE IS FORMED.** When you are ready complete the following Rule Summaries without referring to those pages.

An adjective is a _____ word. It describes, or _____, a noun or _____.

a. There is only one _____ of an adjective.
b. The spelling of an adjective is always in the _____.
c. Most adjectives _____ the _____ they describe.
d. Except that they change their form, a noun and an adjective may be separated by some _____ such as:to ____, to look, to _____, to appear, to _____ and to taste.
e. An adjective of _____ usually follows the measurement noun.
f. When there is more than one adjective describing the same noun, an adjective of _____ usually precedes an adjective of _____.
g. Where there are two or more adjectives of *fact* describing the same noun, they usually come in this order:_____, _____, _____, _____, _____, _____.
_____ then the noun.
Many adjectives are formed from nouns, particularly _____ nouns.
Adjectives often end in _____, _____, _____, _____, al, en, ____ and _____.

Now turn back to pages 19 and 22 to check your answers. Copy the Rule Summaries concerning **THE ADJECTIVE, SOME DETAIL ABOUT AN ADJECTIVE and HOW AN ADJECTIVE IS FORMED** carefully and clearly from those pages.

On the reverse of Card Twelve make additional notes of your own about these points. Copy the *mnemonic* for the order of *adjectives of fact* when they describe the same noun.

CARD THIRTEEN:
Read Pages 22 to 25 about **TYPES OF ADJECTIVE** and when you are ready complete the following Rule Summaries without referring to those pages.

There are _____ types of adjective:
1. Adjectives of _____ *describe* a noun or pronoun.They answer the question
_____ _____ _____?
2. Adjectives of _____ indicate *number* or _____. They answer the question
_____ _____? or *how much?*
3. Adjectives of _____ *set apart* one noun from another noun of the same kind.
There are four kinds of adjective which distinguish.
     A. _____ Adjectives. These answer the question *which?* or *what?*
     B. Possessive Adjectives. These answer the question _____?
     C. Interrogative Adjectives _____ ____ _____ They require a question mark.
     These ask: *Which?* _____? *Whose?*
4. Distributive Adjectives refer _____ to the _____ people or
     items in a group.

Now turn back to pages 25 to check your answers. Copy the Rule Summaries concerning **TYPES OF ADJECTIVE** carefully and clearly from that page.

On the reverse of Card Thirteen discuss each type of adjective giving examples to illustrate your answers.

CARD FOURTEEN:
Read Pages 26 to 28 about **THE COMPARISON OF ADJECTIVES and THE USE OF THE COMPARATIVE AND SUPERLATIVE** and when you are ready complete the following Rule Summaries without referring to those pages.

There are three _____ *of comparison:*
1. The _____ degree involves _____ noun without comparison.
2. The _____ degree compares _____ nouns.
3. The _____ degree is used when more than two nouns are compared.

Adjectives of one syllable:
The *comparative degree* ends in _____. The *superlative degree* ends in _____.
Adjectives of MORE than one syllable: the *comparative* degree is preceded by the word
_____. The *superlative* degree is preceded by the word _____.
There are some irregular adjectives.

Usage:
a. After a comparative we often use _____.
b. A comparative and a _____ are often put together.
c. Use *the* + _____ _____, *the* + *comparative clause* to say that two things
change together or that one thing depends on another.
d. Words such as _____, _____, *a lot,* ___ _____, *rather* and _____

can be used before a comparative.
The superlative:
a. Often, *the* is used with the _____.
b. *By far* and _____ is also used before the superlative.

Now turn back to pages 28 to check your answers. Copy the Rule Summaries concerning **THE COMPARISON OF ADJECTIVE and THE USE OF THE COMPARATIVE AND SUPERLATIVE** carefully and clearly from those pages.

On the reverse of Card Fourteen make any additional notes concerning the comparison of adjectives which you feel will be of benefit to you at school.

CARD FIFTEEN:

Read pages 29 to 37 about **THE PRONOUN** and when you are ready complete the following Rule Summaries without referring to those pages.

A *pro* noun takes the place of a _____ once the _____ has been mentioned in the sentence (or in the context) and it is clear *who* or _____ we are talking about. A pronoun is used to avoid repeating a _____.

There are _____ types of pronoun.

1. _____ Pronouns.   5. _____ Pronouns.
2. _____ Pronouns.   6. _____ Pronouns.
3. Reflexive and _____ Pronouns.   7. _____ Pronouns.
4. _____ Pronouns.

1. A_____ Pronoun is used to replace a noun when it is clear _____ or
   what we are talking about.
2. A Possessive Pronoun shows _____..
3. A Reflexive Pronoun is used when the _____ and the object of the clause or
   sentence are the _____.
   Emphatic Pronouns are _____ pronouns which are used to _____.
4. A Relative Pronoun stands in the _____ part of a sentence. It refers to, and
   tells us more about the _____.
5. An Interrogative Pronoun asks _____.
6. A Demonstrative Pronoun points out or _____ what they stand for.
7. An Indefinite Pronoun takes the place of a _____, thing or place _____.

Now turn back to pages 33 and 37 to check your answers. Copy the Rule Summaries concerning **THE PRONOUN** carefully and clearly from those pages.

On the reverse of Card Fifteen make any additional notes concerning the pronoun which you feel will be of benefit to you at school.

A N S W E R S

Exercise 1
1. table knife fork spoon plate dish
2. girl shop parcels bag
3. teacher books pencils rulers class
4. computer shop
5. briefcase bag umbrella
6. suitcase taxi airport
7. lorry traffic-jam driver delivery shop
8. nursery school picture story song story
9. jigsaw book crayons doll
10. shop factory garage cinema hospital

Exercise 2
1. motorway
2. market
3. mask
4. marmot
5. mason
6. magnet
7. militia
8. magistrate
9. macintosh or mackintosh
10. melody

Exercise 3
1. London and Paris are capital cities.
2. Our school presented the musical, 'Grease', last year. It was a great success thanks to all the hard work put in by Miss Carpenter.
3. The captain of the football team, Barry Brocklehurst, has called a practice for next Tuesday. Can James come?
4. We went to the Grand Canyon in America for our holidays last year.
5. Susy's heart missed a beat as Zak put down his guitar and came towards her.
6. Sara and Jessica went to see Mrs Doubtful at the local cinema last Monday.
7. Brian, Jenny and Shaun are all going to swim at the Oasis Leisure Centre this afternoon in Hunstable. Can Dale come too?
8. What are you wearing to Nicky's party on New Year's Eve?
9. Charley, Harry and Barnaby are just three of Thomasina's kittens.
10. Have you heard the latest releases of Michael Jackson and Wet, Wet, Wet?

Exercise 4
1. Potomac
2. Penines
3. Pacific
4. Pyrenees
5. Paris
6. Paraguay or Peru
7. Pennsylvania
8. Panama
9. Philippines
10. Poland

Exercise 5
1. A pride of lions.
2. A troop of monkeys.
3. A choir of singers.
4. A herd of cows.
5. A swarm of bees.
6. A bouquet (bunch) of flowers.
7. A school of whales.
8. An aviary\flock of birds.
9. A fleet of ships.
10 An army of soldiers.
11. A pack of wolves.
12. A library of books.
13. A gaggle of geese.
14. A shoal of fish.

1. A squadron of clouds.
2. A clowder of cats.
3. A kindle of kittens.
4. A chattering of choughs.

Exercise 6

A	B
love	science
hate	medicine
grief	law
concern	history
anger	religion
spite	geography

C	D
innocence	size
poverty	hardness
guilt	speed
manhood	colour
motherhood	softness
childhood	stickiness

E
discussion
fight
meeting
battle
voyage
decision

Exercise 7
oxen monkeys ponies foxes echoes mice deer cupsful thieves teeth shelves crises lives gulfs dominoes feet atlases calves cargoes radii trolleys wolves babies stories roofs radios rostra gases aircraft geese

Exercise 8

COUNTABLE	UNCOUNTABLE
apple	meat
egg	water
carrot	rice
orange	luggage
book	traffic
handbag	furniture
pamphlet	bread
desk	information
paper	work
cheese	advice

Exercise 9

Words with *a*:	Words with *an*:
song	heir
hoop	orange
house	hour

Exercise 9 contd.

unit	onion
husband	umbrella
hospital	envelope
hamburger	operator
union	ice-cream
university	engineer
unicorn	examination

Exercise 10

COMMON	NEUTER
passenger	sausage
audience	table
swimmer	book
people	paper
pedestrian	window
librarian	curtain
solicitor	house
passer-by	plate
journalist	glass
owner	cup
reader	bed
choir	
cat	
fowl	
child	

MASC.	FEM.
actor	waitress
hero	hostess
bachelor	bride
earl	queen
lord	girl
priest	mother
nephew	wife

Exercise 11

Male	Female	Young
ram	ewe	lamb
stallion	mare	foal
lion	lioness	cub
drake	duck	duckling
hen	cock	chicken
bull	cow	calf
gander	goose	gosling
boar	sow	piglet
buck	doe	leveret
billy goat	nanny goat	kid
dog	bitch	pup

Exercise 12

ic	al	ful
heroic	central	beautiful
athletic	autumnal	careful
metallic	basal	hateful
electric	industrial	spiteful
gigantic	vocal	hopeful

ous		y
courageous		faulty
perilous		mighty
luxurious		wintery
grievious		shadowy
anxious		noisy

Exercise 13

1.   *Most* (quantity) *some* (quantity)
2.   *That* (demonstrative) *my* (possessive)
3.   *Whose* (interrogative) *that (demonstrative)*
4.   *Every* (distributive) *interesting* (quality))
5.   *Six* (quantity) *blue* (quality)

6.   *What* (interrogative)
7.   *Children's* (possessive)
8.   *Several* (quantity) *that* (demonstrative)
9.   *These* (demonstrative) *those* (demonstrative)
10.   *Most* (quantity) *young* (quality) *their* (possessive)

Exercise 14

Positive	Comparative	Superlative
bad	worse	worst
beautiful	more beautiful	most beautiful
slow	slower	slowest
high	higher	highest
cheeky	cheekier	cheekiest
good	better	best
happy	happier	happiest
healthy	healthier	healthiest
exciting	more exciting	most exciting
long	longer	longest
brown	browner	brownest
quick	quicker	quickest
many	more	most
blue	bluer	bluest
wonderful	more wonderful	most wonderful
calm	calmer	calmest
patient	more patient	most patient
little	less	least
considerate	more considerate	most considerate
slow	slower	slowest

Exercise 15

1.	I Ps	myself R	
2.	I Ps	mine Pss	hers Pss
3.	He Ps	me Po	
4.	herself R\E		
5.	I Ps	myself R\E	
6.	I Ps	him Po	
7.	She Ps	me Po	
8.	I Ps	you Po	
9.	themselves R		
10.	ours Pss		

Exercise 16

1.	which A	you Po		
2.	I Ps	myself R\E	you Po	
3.	Which?I	mine Pss	I Ps	that D
4.	whom Ao	you Ps		
5.	This D	that D	Which? I	
6.	who As			
7.	Both Id	I Ps	him Po	
8.	Who? I			
9.	She Ps	me Po		
10.	who A	me Po		